The Shapelessness of Water

The Shapelessness of Water

Poems by

Cheryl Baldi

Kelsay Books

© 2018 Cheryl Baldi. All rights reserved. This material may not be reproduced in any form, published, reprinted, recorded, performed, broadcast, without the express written consent of Cheryl Baldi. All such actions are strictly prohibited by law.

Cover Photograph: Louise Levy
Cover Design: Shay Culligan

ISBN: 978-1-947465-87-9

Kelsay Books
Aldrich Press
www.kelsaybooks.com

In memory of my mother, Marybeth Gotwals Ervin

Acknowledgments

I am grateful to the editors of the following journals in which these poems, some in earlier versions, first appeared: *Bitter Oleander*: "Accident;" *Hands Offering Bread: An Anthology*: "Those Fall Mornings," "Departing;" *Salamander*: "Absence," "Floodwaters," "Trellis," "Upwelling;" *Schuylkill Valley Journal:* "Late into Fall," "What Remains."

I also am grateful to the many friends and writers from both the Bucks County and Warren Wilson writing communities who have been a source of constant inspiration and support. I would like to thank, in particular, Christopher Bursk, Julie Cooper-Fratrik, Judith Ann Levison, Louise Levy, Marcia Pelletiere, and Ethel Rackin. Thanks also to Karen Kelsay and her staff at Kelsay Books. And finally, love and gratitude to my family, especially Eliza, and Meredith, and Rob, always.

Contents

Listen

I. Floodwaters

Floodwaters	19
The Island	20
Frost Warning	21
Intimacy	22
Daybreak	23
Burn	24
Requiem	25
Grace	26

II. Dancer

Accident	29
Dancer	30
War Bride	31
Gunnery Practice	32
Wreck of the Red Arrow, 1947	33
Mad as a Hornet	34
Secrets	35
Red	36
Entering Grief	37
Those Fall Mornings	38
Evening Ritual	39
In the Mood	40
Longing	41
Morning Walk	42
Whose Garden Will This Be?	43
Departing	44

Turbulence	45
New Dwellings	46
Trestle	47
The Body Quits	48

III. Upwelling

Rescue Dive	51
Absence	52
Night Fishing	53
Upwelling	54
Arrhythmia	55
Portrait	57
Compass	58
Calling	59

IV. What Remains

Transience	63
Dusk	64
What Remains	65
Entrance	66
Below the Surface, Snorkeling	67
After Dark	68
Ballooning	69
Late into Fall	70
Ancestors	71

About the Author

*She loved the shore,
the margin, the entrance to
the wild other world. I wept because living
seemed agony to her, and love
the worst.*

—Dana Roeser, *In the Truth Room*

Listen

Think of the sea's cobalt blue
in early morning early fall:

swells coaxed by a steadfast
west wind rise and crest,

plunging suddenly
in a thunder of shore break.

Swirls of white foam
retreat, drawn back

into the next wave and the next,
in and out, each breath in and out.

Breathe

I. Floodwaters

Floodwaters

The air smells of sulfur, and though the storm
is three hundred miles south, on the horizon
dark gray outer bands of clouds spread north.

Along the beach wind crackles and tears
at flags whipping against their poles.
By now, you would have secured the house

and left, hurrying before water rose in the back bays,
swamping docks, flooding roads and homes
of this narrow strip of island you loved and feared

and always returned to. On the last day of your life,
as the nurse closed the window against a threatening sky,
you stared out, listening, as though trying to remember

if you had bolted the upstairs porch door,
or shut off the lights, even as the sea surged
and in a single rush breached the dunes.

The Island

so small we walk it, through spruce
and pine, though this morning
you need to rest
and sit on a stump, alone,
while I make my way to the cliffs,

returning to find you, head bowed,
hands folded in your lap,
meditating, you say,
smiling at the unlikeliness of it.
We know it is your last summer.

At week's end I leave, the ferry
pushing off from the dock
as you stand waving,
your yellow sweater a bright
spot that grows smaller and smaller
against the rocky shoreline

until we turn south, and you disappear,
the wake a path leading back to you,
until it finally ebbs, and all that is left
is the boat, the stern where I stand
looking out at a gray expanse of bay,
swells rocking its green hull.

Frost Warning

You ask that I cover your plants.
It is early fall,
too soon for a freeze,
but you are dying,
and for the second time this week
last night I saw the fox.

Intimacy

Your hand nested in mine.
Your skin the silk of a monarch's wing.

Daybreak

I want to stay, but the nurse
wants your body moved by dawn,
so I kiss your forehead thinking
how few times I've kissed you,
and drive home, sun breaking
over fields through fog.

At home the sky deepens
silver gray to blue.
What woke me, your breathing
unchanged, shallow as a whisper?
What brushed over me?
A breeze from the window.
Your hand stroking my forehead.

Burn

All day the sun beats down
scorching the sand, the streets.
The air is thick and reeks of tar.

In the house I drift from room
to room feeling for a breeze.
Flies hang on the screen,

bite anything. The sea
plummets to a bitter cold.
The beach empties.

Even at night it's too hot to sleep.
Sheets stick, shivers
of sweat drip down my back.

Your death three days old.
Skin to bone, bone to ash.
My head pounds.

Requiem

What I see in the mirror:
your eyes, your dark hair.

What I hear: Brahms, a sustained
f solitary as the late day light,

your footstep down the narrow hall.

Grace

Some nights
you come back.
Tonight
your face
radiant
as the plum
you pick
from a bowl
of jewels.

II. Dancer

Accident

A door swings into her small frame
and a tea pot flies into the air.

What follows: days
deadened by a dark room

her mother's shadow, the doctor's
slow climb up the back steps.

She closes her eyes, scared of his beard
his wheezy voice, her flesh

sticking to the gauze
as it's ripped from her chest

the shapelessness of water
skin and bone

then nothing.

Dancer

She sneaks into the prison
where her father is warden,

a cellblock where an inmate
peers through bars. He hums

deep in his throat. Someone claps.
Another taps his fingers against iron.

The hall echoes with whistles,
cat calls as she begins her dance,

the red plaid of her skirt a blur, her long
skinny legs shadows against concrete.

War Bride

She dreams and dreams:
moonlight, stars spinning

as he pulls her through dunes
to the water's edge.

She wakes: tangled
in a quilt on the floor

confused by the hand on her cheek—
not her husband's, but her mother's

voice whispering.

Gunnery Practice

The war ends, blackouts
lifted, though at night,

out of habit or fear,
she still sits in the dark with her child,

not the boy he wanted
but a girl tucked in her arms.

At dawn the first launch fires
from a boat just off the coast.

All day explosions shake the house,
startle the child by her side.

She sweeps the porch, hangs
sheets on the line to dry, her eyes

scanning the horizon, past
the channel where submarines troll,

stretch of blue water that melts
into blue sky, everywhere she looks

blue and aching,
and in her apron's pocket

the shells she's gathered:
slipper, scallop, dove, whelk,

one for each year he's been gone.

Wreck of the Red Arrow, 1947

It jumps the track, eleven cars,
a blizzard of dust and glass.

As daylight flickers through the eastern slope,
deep in the Alleghenies,

her eyes fix on the rolled
car where she'd been sleeping,

where bodies, wrenched free, are dragged
on blankets up the hill, laid in a bed of snow

head-to-toe along the tracks.
The hillside shudders with what falls:

rock, bone and steel, feathers
from burst pillows, her left shoe.

She stands with the dead
alone under the empty sky, hears

over and over the screams,
her own whispered penance,

the sky close, a dusting of snow
covering it all as though in kindness.

Mad as a Hornet

she is whacking
the shoe against the wall

stunning the damn critter
smacking it again hard

as it hits the floor. Still
the stinger pierces her hand.

She cries in pain
in anger. Her hand swells.

This morning she woke from a dream:
her husband leaving with a woman in a red coat.

Her mother's fallen again.
Her child sulks behind a closed door.

She ices her hand.
For once can't the day go well?

Ticks in the raspberries.
Black swallowtail larvae in the parsley.

Now hornets swarming.
Her husband still not home.

Secrets

First Lorraine, then Lori,
both thin and honeyed,

soft voices that never shut up.
She suspects he's had others, too,

a reminder their failures
are not hers alone.

At night he smokes on the back porch,
gin and orange soda in a glass.

She unmakes the bed, hurls
his shirt into a basket, kicks his shoes

hard under a chair. In the morning
he'll run late trying to find them.

Red

blood from the knife that slips
burst vessel in the eye

her rage her red lipstick
the knife in her hand

bruises on her arm
misshapen scars on her chest

that redden like geraniums
in summer's heat

red the coat he buys his lover
red the coat he buys her

red plums juices
spilling from the tart

the roast carved rare
stunned on the plate.

Entering Grief

She closes the door
   behind her   whispers

alone in the kitchen
   she rocks   whispers

 whispers   and walks in the woods
   she weeps and weeps.

Those Fall Mornings

She yanks at weeds,
stalks of spent lilies,

her husband finally gone,
their child wrapped

in a sweatshirt,
peering over the fence.

She cannot imagine
even the next moment in her life

or later walking to the bay
where the child turns from her.

It's not the sun's glare on the water
but a gust of wind

that is unexpected,
blowing sand

that traps itself in her eye
while the shoreline dissolves,

and goldenrod blooms
against the stillness of blue sky.

Evening Ritual

Her child calls to her,
but she doesn't answer,

alone in the kitchen slicing
cabbage on the oak cutting board.

Onions sizzle, garlic.
She adds a splash of wine.

By the window a shadow.
A memory of her mother stirs.

Leaves rustle, the dead
tiptoeing through the dark.

Her child calls, circling the house,
but she doesn't answer,

alone in the kitchen
learning to savor loneliness.

In the Mood

She dresses in a black
sheath, silver hair swept up,

packs cigarettes,
a lipstick in her clutch.

Men like her, her dark
beauty, her teasing,

her fearlessness
easing into their circle.

At the bar she orders
gin, takes a seat

near the corner
where she can hear

Jelly Roll Morton,
Glenn Miller, horns and reeds,

the long buoyant riffs
like a man's touch

brushing up her spine,
and she's in the mood.

Tonight she will lift up her skirt and dance.
Tonight she will not behave.

Longing

Rain. She opens the window
to listen, imagines

as she lies in the dark
the space beside her emptied

or the weight of another man.
She closes her eyes.

The man by her side
(*who is it?*) moves closer,

but she moves away
listening to the rain's

drum on the metal roof,
the wind's rise and fall

like her own breath, the cool
damp air she draws into her lungs.

The man rests his hand
 in the hollow of her hip,

her skin wet with rain,
the body's memory,

a night long ago, leaves
glistening against black sky.

Morning Walk

She plucks a coin
from the dirt path,

warms it in her hands, holds
safe what another has lost.

When she dies will she have left
enough of herself for each child?

Look, she whispers
to the light piercing the pines.

Stones crackle beneath her step.
A hawk circles and flies off.

She follows the trail of wind,
breath dissolving into light.

Whose Garden Will This Be?

Whose lavender and thyme?

Whose fear?

Whose tomatoes, planted too late,
that finally ripen?

Whose inexhaustible doubt?

Whose kitchen
where rosemary hangs drying?

Whose book open
on the table, in the margin

words scrawled
too faded to read?

Departing

Blue: the tatter of old souls.

The sky beneath which she digs
deep in the dirt, separating roots

hosta iris dry clumps
tangled as despair.

Wrist's blue vein creep
of tinge bluing the lower lip.

In her eyes *forget-me-nots*
bloom constellations blue.

Turbulence

Wind tosses across the yard
scraps of stained curled leaves

as she kneads her hand,
a habit since her stroke.

She aches for warmth, cream
to calm her throat's dry cough.

When she tries to sleep
wind fills her mouth,

and she's hungry for air,
but she can't catch her breath.

New Dwellings

She will live only a few months,
and though her arm shakes

she holds on her lap on a small
round pillow her great-grandson.

He cries, a lamb's bleat,
and her body swells

remembering night's gentle
stretch into the room: her own child

newly born, a warm breeze,
a Luna moth fluttering at the window.

Beneath her the bed creaked,
not lust, but an awakening,

mist of orange and sage, the candle's
saffron flame. Undoing her gown

she'd wept, milk spilling
like a strand of broken pearls

across the ragged rose quilt.

Trestle

She dreams the creek's bank
past the dam where the water

is deep and floods, where once
a girl in a red sweater

was found beneath a canoe.
At the railroad tracks she stops,

listens for the train's whistle
before crossing the trestle

to the meadow. Grasses
untidy and green as moss

sway. She is tired, so tired
and lies in the thickness,

soft as her grandmother's
goose down mattress, the breeze

a cool cloth on her forehead,
her body light as breath,

dissolving in waves,
like contractions.

The Body Quits

An abandoned shell,
a boat she fills

with sea rocket, beach pea,
the wings of monarchs,

sets sail—whelk of pearl
in which she travels with fish.

III. Upwelling

Rescue Dive

At breakfast a man eats poached eggs,
smoked fish, as his wife looks out
past the beach to the blue-green sea.
Waves in a thin white line
break along a distant reef.
In the breeze, a guitar—
notes of regret or sadness
from which the man turns and rises,
sliding into the pool, diving
deep beneath the water's surface
where it is cool, where all he hears
is the sound of his own heart.
On the pool's bottom is a frog
he gathers into the hollow of his hand
and swims, carrying the drowned body
from the pool to place it by a seagrape,
in a nest of wide, flat leaves.
He wants to salvage something,
the tenderness in his hand speaking
for the words he refuses:
the pain in his left shoulder, shame
or fear that causes him to kick in his sleep.
The woman who shares his meals,
hands him a towel, watches,
unsure of who he has become.

Absence

All night bayberry and pines
thrash the house, and its shingles,
worn and curled on the edges,
look black in morning's gray light.
When you left, just past dawn, I waved

and though you waved back, your eyes
were already set on the road ahead.
Inside it was warm, but bewilderingly
empty, our lives filled with too
many things and nothing.

I wanted to call you back, but didn't,
knowing soon you'd cross the bay bridge,
winding through wetlands
where perhaps a lone boat navigates
the small creek inland, past

egrets and brants, the salt shack
we have come to love, long abandoned,
the dock half collapsed, gulls
cluttering the roof, and inside
a broom, a wooden table,
the mattress leaning against the wall.

Night Fishing

We've argued all day,
words heavy as the scent
of Rugosa roses hanging
like dampness in the night air.

While you sleep I listen to the fishermen call.
All night stripers are caught in a deep trough
where currents push and pull
as we push and pull against each other.

Out on the broken water
a tugboat's solitary light,
a sadness over what we've lost,
which I can't even name.

Upwelling

To heal my heart I'm to walk
each day, but this morning,
third day of a land breeze,
it's hot. Still, I set out,
tide low, and by the water's edge
where a fog unfolds, find it's cold.
Following the scrap line
littered with broken shells,
past the stone jetty, I walk,
fog so dense I no longer see
the dunes or houses anchored just beyond,
only the shadow of an early swimmer
in shore break and a gull picking
at a clump of decaying mussels.
I can't tell if the sky is blue
or black any better than I can tell
whether or not I still love you,
but the water and sky suddenly darken
so I turn back, too far from home
if a storm hits, and disappear
into a wall of fog, my life
as unfamiliar as this stretch of beach
I walk every day.

Arrhythmia

What was my father thinking
bringing me a recording of heartbeats
to measure against my own?

For weeks, in the dark
I listened in silence to the 45's
static, it's odd drumbeats.

And when he walked out,
or years later when a man I loved
turned to another how

the heart stammered
in fear. Grief. Even now,
waking from a bad dream,

or plunging in a plane's
steep drop, it stirs, alert
in its struggle to survive,

anguished stuttering,
like the deep breath
it takes to still itself.

Though how much more the heart is.
My friend, at 92, is dying
this late spring afternoon.

The monitor's ticking slows,
his pulse indiscernible,
but he laughs at my bad joke,

then laughs again, surprised
by the sound of his own voice.
It pleases him, as the iris

on the windowsill, as my hand
which he squeezes
with shallow breaths.

And my father who died decades earlier?
What of his heart?
What of his last days

alone in the hospital,
a blizzard keeping us from him?
In truth, I wouldn't have gone

even if I could have.
What of his heart?
And what of my own?

Portrait

An edginess in her face tugs at me,
eyes that catch mine
as she leans over the dirty sink

in the train station's restroom mirror
explaining—*weeks ago a crash, a shattered*
windshield, fragments now shedding.

Under the florescent light her face
glistens, her skin embedded
with what look like diamond chips.

> *diamonds*
> *splinters of stars*

So it is with beauty, its refusal to conceal.
I see in this woman my daughter grown
radiant, but in the eye's crease

some half-wild fear withheld,
her own story unfolding,
certain to cut as quickly as glass.

Compass

How do we learn to forgive what we are asked to forgive?

I can't even forgive the damn compass headings
you've carved into the porch railing. Your east
is my northeast. Northeast is cool, dry winds.

I know this island better than you.
I know where east is.
When I face the sea I face east.

And right now your back is to the east
as we sail on a broad reach across Great Bay,
tacking for the eighth time trying to make our mark,

your stubbornness as fierce
as the currents at tide change and these winds
that keep blowing us off-course.

Again, a gust hurls the boat leeward,
and you with your back to the east,
lean into the wind, your sleight of hand

releasing the sheet so the boat steadies.
Watching you, your shirt rippling
across your broad, straight shoulders,

the way your body knows the wind
as it knows mine, I think, for a moment,
I can forgive anything.

Calling

Knowing she isn't mine
I name her Meredith
guardian from the sea

rock her in hushed swells
of blue water, of silver
light into which I release her:

> *child, my flesh*

circling down
searching among dark shapes
for some deeper resonance

the memory of forgiveness
of fins trembling
the currents' wild dance.

# IV. What Remains

Transience

Late in the day clouds rise
in towers. The sky turns dark
shredded like a worn umbrella.

She loved summer squalls. Winds
swinging to the west. The sea's
sudden flattening to a gray calm.

Today a shelf cloud
spreads over the horizon
rain sweeping through

as the sky breaks apart.
Cool dry air sinks down
and you, restless cloud,

blown where?

Dusk

A ritual to sit each night in teak chairs
weathered to gray. On the dune's slope
we'd count waves or the night's first stars,

by August, Perseid showers streaking
seaward: the more we counted,
the closer to summer's end.

But tonight dusk rustles with life.
A fisherman hauls in another blue.
A boy in red trunks kicks at the water's edge,

every seventh wave larger than the rest
she told me, and I keep counting, wondering
what else she said that I've forgotten.

What Remains

By November it turns cold.
I pack away linens, the brass bell,
empty cabinets of food
though already mice have moved in.

Salt mixes with the scent of Peky cypress,
and in every room her presence
left from decades of opening and closing
the house, seasons of winter storms,

one northeaster that cut the island in two.
For weeks we thought the house was gone,
but found it standing, the north corner
collapsed, roof and doors torn off.

We picked through rubble, found
driftwood, an old glass
she filled with shells:
a lesson in beginning again.

Coming back each spring
to sand pressed against the house,
crevices beneath the porch
where water rushed during spring tides,

I unboard windows, shovel
fill around footings, grateful,
though she is gone, the house
remains, and in its emptiness

holds her, as she once held
a skate's egg sack,
hesitating, before tossing it
back to the sea.

Entrance

The wildness here set her free:
always wind, always the waves'
refusal to hold their shape.

She taught me to find the deep
channels that rush from the shoreline,
emptying out into the larger sea.

In rough water one can ride them
straight through the breakers, a secret
passage to another world

where one becomes part
of something larger, endless
sweep of blue sky, endless sea

beneath which swells
life unknown, and dangerous,
and thriving.

Below the Surface, Snorkeling

Sun shimmers across a sandy flat
through sea grasses and beyond
to where the reef stands like a pillar.

A school of blue tangs cluster
at the cave's mouth. Sea fans, too,
pulsing back and forth
in the current's flow.

All sound muted, only
the soft, dull rasp of breath
in and out through the narrow tube.

After Dark

Gone are the hydrangeas my grandmother planted
and the roses, though silver lace
still creeps along the wall beneath the scrub pine,

and inside the house not much has changed:
scent of cedar, bowls of dusty shells,
a deck of weathered cards.

Five generations have eaten on these same plates,
from the same serving bowls,
which tonight hold spaghetti, mussels.

In an old photograph: my grandparents
in their straw hats; the annual house party they hosted—
women in shirtwaist dresses, men in ties, smoking.

In another: the woman who became my step mother,
my father smiling at her, my mother by his side,
her dark hair blown back from her face.

And I think they *were happy* that day, and many others,
though what seeped in—those common griefs—broke us all.
Tonight, my children and grandchildren are here,

each with our own story, but as we clear plates
and crack open more wine for a game of rummy,
those out for an evening walk will pass by

and see us gathered around this long table,
candles lighted, the chandelier swaying, screens
crusted with salt, the hard north wind easing.

Ballooning

My daughter visits.
We eat late, then read,

the night air still,
but in the quiet, suddenly

she stirs, a puzzled look:
specks of silver,

like dust floating in the air.
We look closer.

Tiny tinseled threads,
glittering in the lamp's light,

unroll from the beams,
as the room fills

with the gauzy lacework
of newborn webs.

My daughter, on her feet,
leans into the light.

Oh, she says.
And again, *Oh,*

which is all I can say
each time I see her face.

Late into Fall

Tomatoes, sun-ripened and fat,
sliced thin with onion on bread,
September's late sweet corn—
the week she died it's all we ate

in silence at the long table
as winds shifted west
hushing the sea, so it seemed
a lake, deep blue and forgiving.

Here the water stays warm late into fall,
and all she loved—bittersweet
bloom of goldenrod,
the wolf spider's orb this morning

stretching from lamp post
to bayberry, flecked with gnats
and dew from a fog so dense
it's obscured everything—

unfolds, as the sun rises
and burns the mist, so the beach,
emptied and swept clean,
comes to light, rocks,

sea grasses, sea and sky
unending, and for now, any sadness
or regret is released into this
dazzling, metallic-silver light.

Ancestors

Sun glints through the chairs' curved backs.

    Spindles of light spread long over the table.

        At dinner I sit facing the sea.

Tonight terns skim the sea's flat surface

    for bait fish. A crab

        wrenched from the tide's scrap line.

Evening stills, a hush of dragonflies' meshed wings.

    In the waves' folding a lullaby of voices,

        those I've loved, the night's first stars.

About the Author

Cheryl Baldi is a graduate of the Warren Wilson MFA Program for Writers, a former Bucks County Poet Laureate, and a finalist for the Robert Fraser Award for Poetry. Her work has appeared widely in journals, including *Bitter Oleander*, for which she was a finalist in the 2006 Francis Locke Memorial Award and *Salamander*, which nominated her work in 2008 for the Best New Poets anthology. She served on the faculty of Bucks County Community College for 25 years teaching writing and literature, has worked as a free-lance editor, and served as co-facilitator for community based workshops exploring women's lives through literature. She lives with her husband in Bucks County, Pennsylvania.